Baskets

Projects, techniques and inspirational
designs for you and your home

Tabara N'Diaye

Photography by Penny Wincer
Illustrations by Aurelia Lange

Hardie Grant

QUADRILLE

Maman, Mamy, Grand-Mère – trois générations de femmes inspirantes sans qui cette aventure n'aurait pas été possible.

Mum, Mamy, Grandma – three generations of inspirational women without whom this journey would not have been possible.

Publishing Director Sarah Lavelle
Jnr. Commissioning Editor Harriet Butt
Copy Editor Gillian Haslam
Design and Art Direction Gemma Hayden
Photographer Penny Wincer
Illustrator Aurelia Lange
Prop Stylist Nuala Sharkey
Production Director Vincent Smith
Production Controller Sinead Hering

The publisher wishes to thank A New Tribe for
their generous loan of props for the photo shoot.

Published in 2019 by Quadrille, an imprint
of Hardie Grant Publishing

Quadrille
52–54 Southwark Street
London SE1 1UN
quadrille.com

Cataloguing in Publication Data: a catalogue record for
this book is available from the British Library.

ISBN 978 1 78713 270 2

Printed in China

Contents

Introduction

When I was growing up in Paris, as soon as the last school bell rang in late June, my brother, sister, mother and I immediately hopped on a flight to Dakar, the capital of Senegal, West Africa, for our annual summer holiday. Leaving behind us the bustling streets of the French capital, we'd head for a place where the sun is always shining and, most importantly, to be reunited with family.

I always loved our time in the city of Dakar, admiring the huge display of pink bougainvillea flowers on the façades of houses, spending lazy afternoons at the beach, drinking large glasses of *bissap* (a local drink made from dried hibiscus flowers) or hailing a *calèche* (a horse-drawn cart) on a busy road. But it was always when we headed to Thiès, my parents' hometown and an hour's drive inland from Dakar, and pushed open the grey door to my grandmother's house, with the mango tree right in the middle of the courtyard, that I felt right at home.

I'd walk through Thiès, soaking up the liveliness and colours of the markets, and to this day I'm still fascinated by all the artisans, busy at work and selling all kinds of craft under the blazing sun. With their eclectic spread, basket stands were always the first stalls to catch my attention

(and my pocket money). Some tall, some small, some with lids like turrets and others with vibrant colours running through their patterns…

I also loved the fact that they were all handcrafted by women, and I quickly learned that this was a craft passed down from generation to generation by women in rural villages. Watching them weave at the speed of light was absolutely mesmerizing, and there was a unique sense of community and joy amongst them.

As a teenager, I started buying and using these beautiful Senegalese baskets made from local grasses and coloured strings for anything and everything – jewellery, make-up, laundry. Years later, when I was fitting out my first flat and looking for storage with personality, I knew exactly where to go! These baskets were like a beautiful memory box, stimulating precious recollections of people, places and times gone by.

In 2017, I teamed up with my sister to launch La Basketry, our homeware brand designed in collaboration with a group of female basket-weavers from Ngaye Mkeke, a small village outside Thiès, who we've got to know and love over the years. And the same year, I finally

learned how to weave baskets – something I had longed to do for years. I initially taught myself by deconstructing baskets, before learning different techniques at school in London and on the ground in Senegal. I was instantly hooked!

Leading a busy life in a hectic city, basket-making peacefully allows me to zone out. Hours pass while all I care about is transforming some grasses into a beautiful object, forgetting about my phone and my to-do list and just focusing on the present moment. Sure, not everything turns out perfectly – I've had my fair share of broken needles and odd-shaped baskets, but I enjoy the process so much.

Meanwhile, baskets are becoming more and more popular. No longer confined to the kitchen, basket walls are pinned everywhere on the internet, basket lampshades have been hailed as the interior trend *du jour*, and woven basket bags are toted by stylish ladies around the world all year round. However, there has always been a stigma attached to basketry – despite baskets being super popular, the craft itself is still seen as 'too elaborate', 'too complex', 'time consuming' or even 'requiring a lot of space'.

The reality is that there are so many different techniques, some simpler than others, and there's an abundance of materials available (did you even know that you can make baskets out of yarns, newspapers or even plastic bags?) and that just as with any other craft, the old saying of 'Practise Makes Perfect' holds true.

This book is my way of shining a light on this traditional craft, with contemporary designs for the modern home and the modern maker. My collection of projects will enable you to be creative and experiment with different colours, patterns and materials, plus there are useful tips on how to decorate your home with them.

Basketry is already at the heart of your home – it's woven into your DNA!

Tabara x

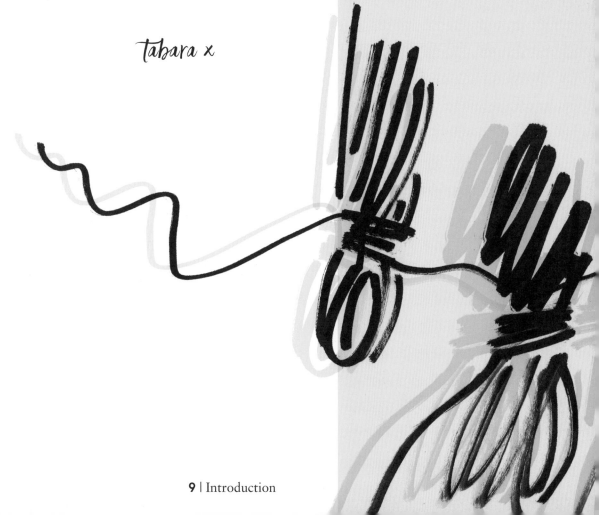

History + culture

Delving into the world of basketry is fascinating. It is considered to be one of the world's most ancient crafts, although it is difficult to date its exact origins as many of the vegetable materials used to weave baskets are perishable. However, according to archaeologists, the oldest known baskets are probably 10,000 to 12,000 years old and were found in the Egyptian Pyramids.

For this reason, it's not surprising to learn that many other crafts have roots in basketry. Pottery is one such craft – baskets were used as moulds and lined with clay; when it had dried out, the clay bowl was then used for cooking food. Another example is the craft of fabric-weaving – the method of interlacing grasses into fine strips was later employed when weaving materials such as wool, flax or cotton.

What's even more fascinating is that every civilization in every part of the world has practised basketry at some point in its history. Men and women have always had at their disposal materials such as leaves, woods and grasses that naturally lend themselves to the construction of baskets – the broad definition of a basket being 'a receptacle made of interwoven material'. Historically, baskets were primarily used as an agricultural tool to process and store grain and carry food, but were also used in fishing and presented as wedding gifts.

The materials used for weaving were determined by the plants native to the regions where they were being made. Bamboo and canes have always been used in abundance in South-east Asia, while palm, banana and sisal leaves

were and still are more popular in Africa. And as explorers discovered new worlds and as populations migrated from one country to another, baskets were easily traded across geographic and social borders. This also explains how basketry techniques have travelled around the world, for example West African techniques of coiling were carried over to the Americas.

Basket-making around the world
While basket-making has long been celebrated around the world, I've chosen to highlight some key cultures and their use of baskets past or present.

Asia
From the instantly recognizable basket boats of Vietnam to the conical triangular hats worn across the continent, there's a wide diversity of basketry products available across Asia. Canes and bamboos are the king materials, with Japan growing more than a hundred varieties of bamboo and centre cane heavily exported to the US and Europe. Bamboo baskets have evolved from being an everyday necessity of rural life to being celebrated and holding a special place in culture, for example becoming integral in tea ceremony rituals.

Europe
Willow is often recognized as the first material of Europe although, due to its cost, basket-makers frequently used other wild plants that could be freely gathered from woods and hedgerows. Willow growing and weaving are labour intensive, and the major European basket-making industries in Eastern Europe

In the village of Ngaye Mkeke, Senegal, basket-makers gather in courtyards to weave baskets from local grasses and long, colourful strings.

Patterns are added in the form of decorative bands, geometric shapes and different colours, while the core material can be left in its natural state – this technique is called 'exposed core'.

are facing stiff competition from Asia. Willow is harvested annually in winter or spring before the sap rises, and preparing willow involves soaking it for a period that can vary from a couple of hours up to 10 days.

America

Native American basketry was one of the first crafts to be commercially exploited and it became a major trade item due to its bright colours and intricate patterns. These baskets were also desirable due to their decoration, which could involve the use of stones and feathers, mollusc shells cut into beads and pendants, and the use of natural dyes. It is impossible to talk about basket-weaving in America without mentioning the West African slaves who brought the coiling techniques to some of the southern states. Slaves discovered that palmetto leaves and grasses were similar to those used in Africa and wove beautiful baskets that played a key role in rice cultivation on plantations.

Africa

In a continent of over 50 countries, there's an infinite variety of basket types, from the palm-leaf shoppers of Marrakesh to sisal and raffia baskets from Ghanaian villages, and obviously my beloved Senegalese baskets. Basket-making is still a form of employment for many African women and many basketry cooperatives have been set up in rural areas, bringing vital additional income to populations and keeping the craft alive. Back in Senegal, coiled baskets are now woven using long recycled plastic strings that makers obtain from nearby factories. In South Africa, baskets have been woven with recycled telephone wire, while in Gambia strips cut from plastic bags provide a new use for a material that would have once been thrown away.

Basket-making today

Basket-making has been adopted and adapted but never abandoned around the world. From the wicker chairs at your favourite café to the straw hat you rock every summer, this craft is showing no sign of being woven out.

There may be fewer skilled makers than there once used to be, but as consumers continue to move away from mass-produced items towards artisan-crafted products with a story and a person behind them, the basket made from natural materials and with an environmentally-friendly message fits right in.

How to use this book

Like many other crafts, mastering the art of basketry will enable you to create beautiful and decorative objects, but the real beauty of basket-making is in the fact that these items are practical and can be used around the home as part of your everyday life.

When you realize how accessible basket-making is and that not too many tools are needed – the most important ones being your hands – you'll want to learn the craft immediately and this is exactly what this book will show you! You do not need any prior experience, but if you are already a crafter this will help as you will see how basketry is intertwined with so many other disciplines such as sewing, weaving or shaping in pottery. However, if you're a total craft newbie and haven't attempted anything artistic since school, please don't worry as each project is explained in simple steps, and there are some very easy beginner projects, too.

This book takes you on a journey, introducing you to the history of baskets and how this craft has evolved throughout the centuries to what it is today, via a wide range of projects. Taking inspiration from the Senegalese baskets I fell in love with when I was younger and the first technique I played around with, the opening chapter *Grass* (see pages 20–71) is an homage to those coiled baskets, achieved by wrapping plastic strings with a needle around the core material – a bundle of grasses.

The *Cane* chapter (see pages 72–105) will appeal to you if you like getting your hands dirty – literally – as it involves soaking the centre cane, bending it, then reshaping to create everything from a picnic basket to a decorative tray for your coffee table.

The third chapter on *Rope* (see pages 106–121) demonstrates a modernized version of the coiling technique featured in the first chapter, but here a regular needle has been replaced by a sewing machine.

And to complete the projects, the *Twine* chapter (see pages 122–140) employs a similar weaving technique to cane, but the rolls of twine are softer, kinder to your hands and come in an impressive range of colours, allowing you to be very creative.

Each chapter includes instructions on how to make a basic basket using the relevant material. Don't skip these introductory projects as they will enable you to familiarize yourself with the materials, techniques, terminology and, most importantly, get you creating right away. Once you have mastered these introductory projects, you're ready to go and can start tackling more advanced baskets.

Measurements are provided as a guideline. Exact dimensions and quantities depend on your dexterity and your tension when you weave –

your work may end up being tighter or looser, so please always factor in some leeway when sourcing materials for your projects.

Most of the projects in this book have simplified aesthetics so you can really focus on the techniques, but once you've perfected them, let your imagination run wild and allow your personality and your own style to shine through! Dye some cane, paint the bottom of your rope basket or replace the plastic strings in the coiled baskets with some fabric!

As a final word, be kind to yourself and try to be patient as your skills will improve day by day – I'm still learning every day. As they say, practise makes perfect. If you focus on loving the process rather than just the results, you'll be building a hobby that will provide joy throughout your life.

Materials

Choosing the right materials is an essential part of basketry because it determines the technique you use.

Plastic strings
Growing up in France, I used these 'scoubidou' strings to make everything from friendship bracelets to rainbow key chains. They are easy to buy online (and sometimes described as plastic lacing cord) and usually come as pre-cut 1-m (39-inch) lengths in packs of 50 or 100 strings, either in just one colour or an assortment of colours.

Centre cane
Centre cane is a round cane made from the inside of the rattan palm, imported from South-east Asia. It comes in bundles and can be purchased in a variety of sizes (see the chart on page 75 for the sizes used in my projects).

Centre cane is too brittle to be woven in its dry state, so you will need to soak it first in lukewarm water to make it easier to manipulate. See page 91 for information on soaking times.

Sisal and jute twine
Made from natural plant fibres, you may already have rolls of sisal and jute twine around the home and garden as they are often used when wrapping presents, tying up plants, or for meat preparation and general kitchen use. Sisal twine is stiff and rough textured, making it perfect to act as the core material when twining, while jute twine is softer and comes in a rainbow of colours.

Cotton rope
Soft, smooth and braided rope made from 100% cotton is my preferred type of cord to work with and will give a smooth finish to your baskets.

Cotton rope comes in different thickness, but a 6–8mm diameter (approx ¼ inch) is what you will require for the projects in this book. It can be purchased in cut lengths, but it is definitely more cost-effective to buy a whole roll of 50 or 75m (55 or 80 yards).

Grass
There are many natural grasses found in and around the garden that can be harvested and prepared for basket-weaving. Depending on where you live and the time of the year, hard rush, pendulous sedge, reed, sweetgrass, pine needle, hay, wheat bunch or skep-making straw are all good options, but really any dried grass will work.

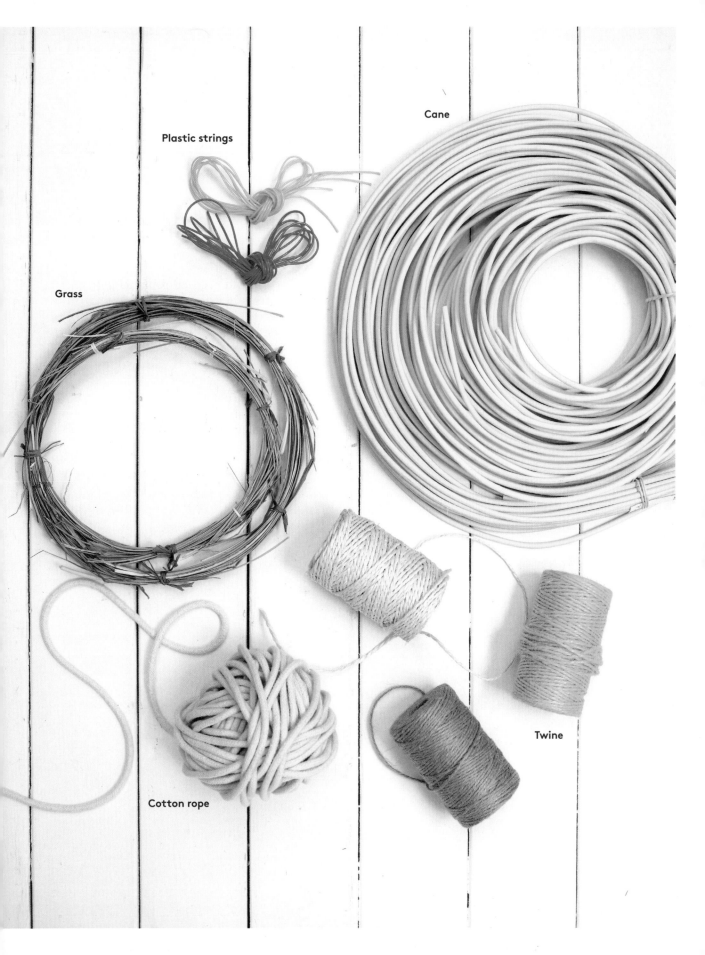

Plastic strings

Cane

Grass

Cotton rope

Twine

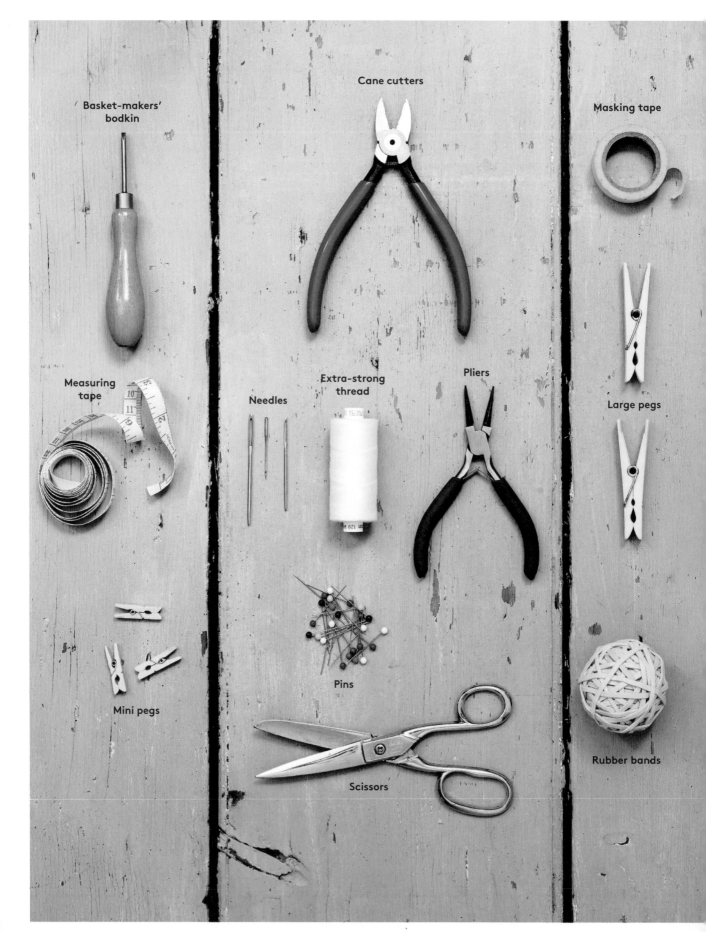

Cane cutters

Basket-makers' bodkin

Masking tape

Measuring tape

Needles

Extra-strong thread

Pliers

Large pegs

Mini pegs

Pins

Rubber bands

Scissors

Equipment

There are only a few specialist tools you will need to get your basket-making journey started, and you may already have some of these in your home.

Basket-makers' bodkin The essential tool when working with cane and very handy for other materials, too. It is used to pierce through the cane when creating a base and to make gaps to help weave the cane in.

Cane cutters Essential for cutting centre cane. Useful with other materials too.

Masking tape I'm a big fan of masking tape and it's ideal for securing purposes. It's very convenient to have a roll when working with grasses, to keep them in a bundle.

Measuring tape Essential for measuring lengths of cane, rope, twine and to keep an eye on the size and height of each project.

Needles You will need different types of needles. Weaver's needles and large-eyed needles are perfect for thicker materials like grasses and natural fibres. Strong needles like jeans or leather ones are ideal when working with cotton rope, and stock up as you're likely to break one or two!

Extra-strong thread Used with leather or jeans needles for rope projects, this is a must-have (available from most craft shops).

Pliers Essential when working with cane to pinch stakes and bend them upwards to start shaping and working the sides of a basket.

Clothes pegs and clips The clothes pegs/clothes pins or little clips are key when working with grasses or twine to hold your project in place as you work, as you don't want your coiling (for the grasses) or twining (for the twine) to completely unravel. The pegs are also great to hang up dyed cane and let it dry.

Scissors Every crafter has a pair of scissors in their kit! Just make sure they are sharp so you can snip through the different materials without difficulty.

Pins I like to use pins with coloured heads as they are easier to see when inserted into the basket being woven.

Rubber bands and string Rubber bands are good for tying up twine as they are a soft material. Strong string will work for cane.

Extra bits
Sewing machine For rope projects, you need a sewing machine with zigzag stitch.

Bucket Centre cane is too brittle to be woven in its dry state, so needs to be soaked in a bucket of lukewarm water to make it easier to manipulate without breaking.

Craft knife Always use it carefully – cut away from the hand holding the material. A flat knife and a sharp knife are used to cut grasses.

Weights Perfect to hold down your basket when working with cane or twine.

Grass

Grass

There's something quite rustic and traditional about basket-making with grasses, as historically baskets were created with either natural woods and/or grasses.

Any dried grass will work for the projects in this chapter, including sea bent grass, marram grass, oat straw, soft rush, sweetgrass and sedge. It is important that whatever material you use has been thoroughly dried out before use as freshly cut grasses will shrink when drying out and this will affect your finished project. Late autumn and early spring are the optimal times of the year to harvest grasses – they should always be fairly tall with long stems.

If, like me, you live in a city and are not able to collect your own wild grass, there are many excellent online suppliers of grasses, or why not pop down to your nearest garden centre to explore the various options available? However, if you're still struggling to find a good grass option, a good alternative is raffia. Available in most craft shops, this is cost-effective and can be purchased in its natural colour or in a variety of bright colours.

When working with grasses, the main technique is referred to as 'coiling'. Coiling is often described as 'a sewing technique that consists of sewing a spiral foundation of grass securely in a coil and wrapping this coil with another material that is threaded through a needle and sewn over the coils'. This makes it sound harder than it is, so see pages 24–27 for the basic technique which is easy to master once you have practised a few times.

Grass how to

This section will guide you through some of the basics of weaving a coiled basket using grasses – how to start your base, join in new core material and new stitching material, shaping and finishing your basket.

1. Gather 10 pieces of core material into a bundle 1.3cm (½ inch) in diameter, with cut ends level. Hold the bundle one thumb's width from the end and secure tightly with plastic string in an overhand knot (see page 27). Thread a needle with plastic string. Start coiling the bundle into a flat circle around the knot, stitching through the centre of the coil to keep the grass in place.

2. Continue to coil a circle, stitching the plastic string through the core material in the previous row. The stitches are about 5mm (¼ inch) apart. Once the first couple of rows are completed, it becomes easier as you have more material to grip. For a flat base, make sure the coils are side by side.

1

2

3. When the bundle of core material thins out, join in more grasses simply by adding more strands into the bundle to keep the diameter of the bundle consistent.

4. When you're left with only a short length of plastic string (or whatever stitching material you are using), thread the end into the previous row. Join in a new length of string by threading it a couple of wraps back (you may have to hold it in place while you make the next couple of stitches to ensure it stays secure).

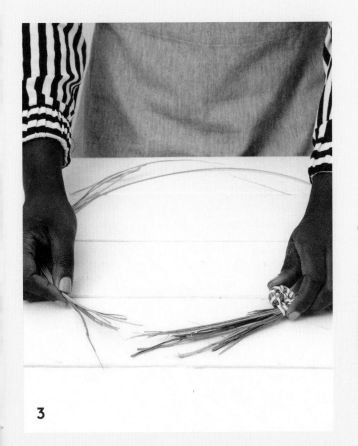

3

4

5. To shape your basket or bowl and to build up the sides, place the coils directly on top of the previous circle. Make sure you are holding the core material in the correct place and using each stitch to hold it there. As you build up the sides, make sure the sides are straight and not leaning in the wrong direction.

6. To finish, trim a few strands of the core material, so the bundle becomes thinner in diameter. Finish your last row by wrapping the plastic string tightly into the core material so that it won't unravel.

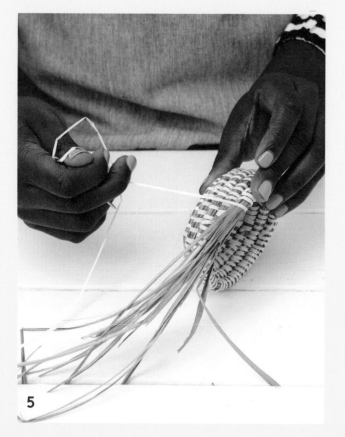

5

6

How to make an overhand knot

This simple knot is the starting point when coiling grass (see step 1, page 24), and is used to attach your stitching material to the bundle of grass (known as the core material).

1. To make an overhand knot, wrap your string around the bundle and hold both ends on one side of the bundle – you want the left end to be about 5cm (2 inches) long.

2. Cross the left end over the right end, creating a loop, then pass it under (through the loop) and pull tightly.

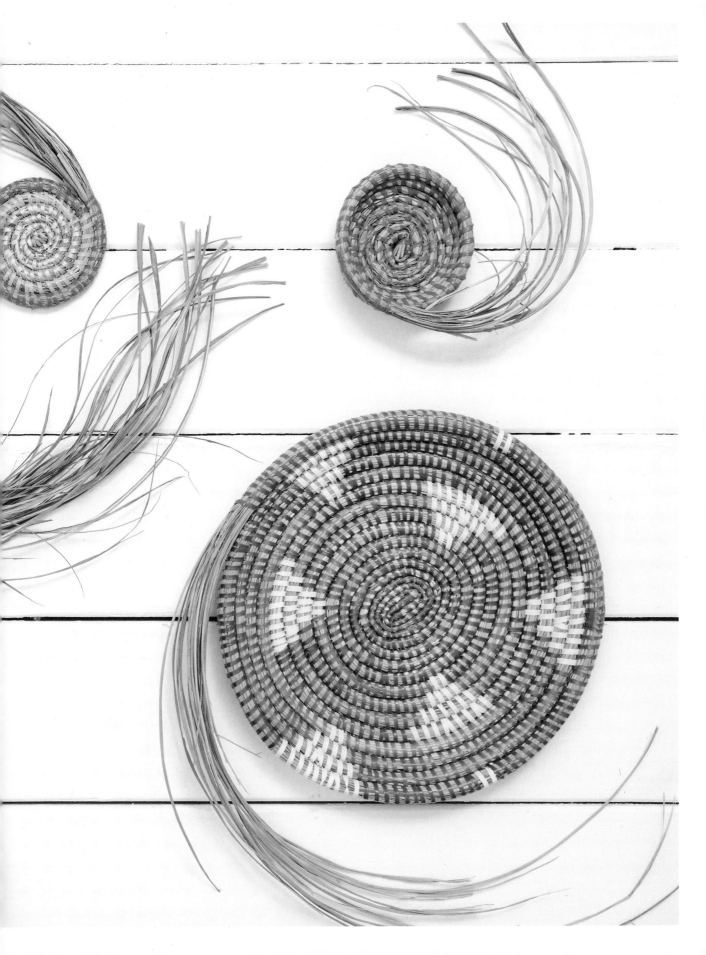

Drinks coasters

Whether you're drinking your morning coffee or enjoying a cocktail with friends, these simple coiled coasters are just what you need and make the perfect project for beginner basket-weavers.

Materials (per coaster):
1.2-m (47-inch) lengths of core material (dried grass of your choice or raffia), making a bundle 1.3cm (½ inch) in diameter (this will be approx 10 pieces)
4 x 1-m (39-inch) lengths of white plastic string
Large-eyed needle
Ruler or measuring tape
Scissors

I love the simplicity of this project as it really allows the coiling technique to shine through.

1.   Hold your core material one thumb's width from the bundle ending and tie the plastic string around it in an overhand knot, securing it tightly (see page 27). Thread a needle through the plastic string to prepare for stitching.

2.   Start forming the bundle in a circle (in the direction which is more comfortable to you) around the knot, stitching through the centre (see step 2, page 24) – this is the trickiest bit, so don't be discouraged if at first it seems a bit difficult!

3.   Continue forming a circle, wrapping the bundle around the inner coil and stitching the plastic string through the core material in the previous row. This becomes easier once the first couple of rows are completed, as you have more material to grip. Try to maintain an even tension for a perfectly rounded coaster (and to avoid a misshapen finished piece!). If the circle becomes a bit wonky, gently manipulate it back into a circle (grasses are quite easily to manipulate, but this become more difficult as the circle grows, so it is very important to keep an eye on the first few rows of coiling).

4.   When the bundle thins, join in more core material simply by adding the strands into the bundle and wind over it strongly (see step 3, page 25). You need to ensure the bundle has a consistent diameter so that your coaster ends up an even thickness (and to avoid your mug or glass wobbling on it).

5.   When you're left with only a short length of plastic string, join in new stitching material (see step 4, page 25).

6.   Stitch your coaster until it measures approx 9cm (3½ inches) in diameter, or until you have 6–8 concentric rows. Finish off by threading the plastic string into the previous row several times, then cross stitch it to the previous row to secure.

7.   Trim off any excess materials, and your first coaster is done! Repeat to create a set, using different colours of string if you wish.

Two-tone placemats

Dress your dining table with these two-tone placemats to make your everyday meals and your next dinner party, events to remember! Making a set of mats is the perfect way to continue to perfect your base while starting to play with patterns and using a range of colours to complement your home.

Materials (per placemat):
11m (12 yards) of your preferred core material, making a bundle 1.5cm (⅝ inch) in diameter
20 x 1-m (39-inch) lengths of black plastic string
20 x 1-m (39-inch) lengths of white plastic string
2 large-eyed needles
Ruler
Scissors

1. Gather 10–12 strands of your preferred dried material for the core of your placemat, making a bundle 1.5cm (⁵⁄₈ inch) in diameter and 1 black plastic string for the stitching material, and begin a round base with 6 rows (see steps 1 and 2, page 24).

2. Start row 7 with the black stitching material but instead of doing a full row, do a half row, resembling a half moon.

3. Now start following the two-toned pattern shown below.

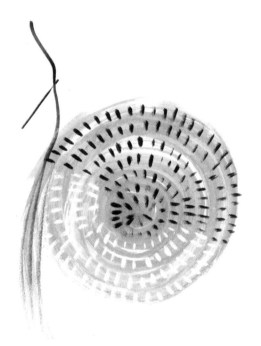

4. Join in a white plastic string with your second needle and begin stitching at a point between two wrappings of the previous round to complete the second half moon and row 7.

5. Now take back your first needle with the black plastic string and start row 8, working again on half a row.

6. As before, use the white plastic string to stitch the second half of the row.

7. Join in new core material and stitching materials where necessary (see steps 3 and 4, page 25).

8. Continue working, following the two-tone pattern until your placemat is the desired size – for use with dinner plates, a practical diameter is 28cm (11 inches), or 16–18 two-toned rows.

9. For the last full row, trim off a few strands of grass to create a thinner bundle. Use your second needle with the black string for the last time and wrap half a row onto the previous row. To wrap the final outer row more tightly and to make your work more secure, wrap back using the same stitch holes in the reverse direction, resulting in a double-wrapped rim, which adds strength and creates an X design on the border. Repeat with white string on the other side of the placemat. Fasten off the white string and trim off any excess materials at the point where the black stitching starts.

To keep coils the same thickness, try feeding them through a small round cookie cutter the same diameter as your bundle. When the bundle no longer fills the cookie cutter, add more grass.

Mini baskets

Perfect for storing loose coins, keys, jewellery or even mini succulents, these small-scale baskets look great lined up on a shelf or grouped together on a bedside table, plus this is an easy and fun project to make once you've perfected your base and shaping skills.

Materials:
2m (2¼ yards) of your preferred core material, making a bundle 1.5cm (⅝ inch) in diameter
5 x 1-m (39-inch) lengths of plastic string in colours of your choice
Large-eyed needle
Ruler or measuring tape
Scissors

If using a different stitching material, make sure it doesn't snap as this is frustrating. Good-quality raffia, handspun linen threads and fabric yarn are great options.

1. Gather 10–12 strands of your preferred dried material into a bundle 1.5cm (⅝ inch) in diameter for the core of your basket and 1 black plastic string for the stitching material and begin a round base (see steps 1 and 2, page 24).

2. When you have worked 6 rows of stitching and have a solid base, you can start to coil up the sides of the basket in order to shape it.

3. Continue working in a spiral, but start row 7 by placing coils directly on top of another (see step 5, page 26). The stitching continues as before, and make sure you are holding the core material in the correct place and using each stitch to hold it there.

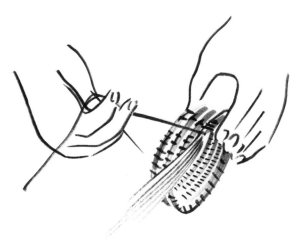

4. Continue working round and keep a close eye on the shape from different angles and on your tension for an even basket. Work the sides up for 6 rows.

5. Start row 7 with the black string, but only do half a row. Fasten off the black string by threading it into the previous row.

6. Change the colour by joining in a green string (see step 4, page 25), securing it in place by threading it in a couple of rows back (you may need to hold it in place while you do your first few stitches). Work 2 rows (rows 8 and 9) of stitching.

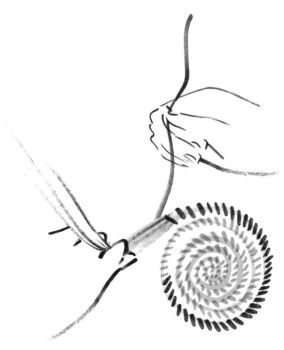

7. To finish your mini-basket, trim a few strands of the core material to make the bundle a little thinner and finish row 10 by wrapping the stitching material tightly into the core material. Trim off any excess materials.

Shelfie inspiration

'So, where's the starfish from?' I love how a shelfie always works as a conversation starter when people visit my home.

More decorative than functional, there are no rules to what can and cannot go on a shelf, but here are some of my top tips:

1. Keep it tonal – although a small pop of colour can be very effective. Pick a colour scheme that sits well within the room and stick to it.

2. Play around with textures to add visual interest and dimension, like the textured background against the white wall or the empty gold frame.

3. Vary heights so the eye can scan your shelfie properly – baskets are perfect for this as they come in all sizes and shapes, but glass bottles and ceramics are also great additions.

4. Bring a little life to your display with some greenery. We all know that plants can bring a sense of calm to any room and even purify the air around us.

5. Add something unusual, like this beautiful starfish I picked up while travelling the world.

And lastly, always take one thing away from the display once you've styled it!

Triangle pattern bowl

Eye-catching and unique with its triangular motif, this modern coiled bowl will make a sophisticated addition to your home.

Materials:
12m (13¼ yards) of your preferred core material, making a bundle 1.5cm (⅝ inch) in diameter
20 x 1-m (39-inch) lengths of green plastic string
20 x 1-m (39-inch) lengths of white plastic string
2 large-eyed needles
Ruler or measuring tape
Scissors

1. Gather 10–12 strands of your preferred dried material for the core of your basket, making a bundle 1.5cm (⁵⁄₈ inch) in diameter, and 1 green plastic string for the stitching material. Make a round base with 7 rows (see steps 1 and 2, page 24).

2. Now start following the triangle pattern shown below, for the three triangles in the base of the bowl. Start row 8 of the coil with the green stitching material but instead of doing a full row, do 18–20 stitches.

3. Join in a white string using the second needle and do 2 stitches – these 2 stitches will be the base of your first triangle.

4. Revert back to your first needle and do 18–20 stitches in green, followed by 2 stitches in white.

5. Repeat step 4 – you have now completed row 8 and have the base for the three triangles. These should be spaced equidistantly around the bowl.

6. Start row 9 by stitching in green until you reach the 2 white stitches from the 8th row. Add 4 white stitches to continue building the triangle shape, then revert back to green. Repeat until you have completed the row.

7. Repeat step 6, this time adding 7 white stitches until row 10 is completed.

8. Repeat step 6, this time adding 10 white stitches until you have completed row 11. You have now completed your first three triangles.

9. Your next three triangles will be positioned in between the first three triangles, plus you are now going to coil up the sides and shape the basket by placing rows directly on top of one another (see step 5, page 26).

10. Start row 12 with a green string and do 34 stitches – your last stitch should be in between the last 2 rows of white stitching. Join in a white string and do 2 white stitches that will act as the base of the 4th triangle. Continue alternating 34 green stitches and 2 white stitches until you have completed a full row and have the bases of your 4th, 5th and 6th triangles.

11. Repeat step 6 with 4 white stitches.

12. Repeat step 7 with 7 white stitches.

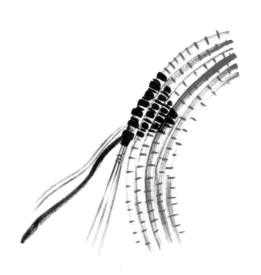

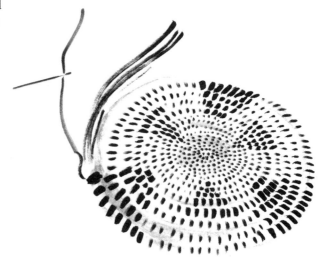

13. Repeat step 8 with 10 white stitches. You have now completed your 4th, 5th and 6th triangles.

14. You are now going to create the 7th, 8th and 9th triangles. As before, you want the 7th triangle be in the middle of the 4th and 5th triangles, so stitch in green for 40–42 stitches (depending on your tension), then add 2 white stitches.

15. Repeat until you have completed the base of the 7th, 8th and 9th triangles.

16. Repeat steps 11–13 to complete the final 3 triangles.

17. Once you've completed the 9th triangle, revert back to green stitching for a whole row. You have now completed the sides of your basket and can finish with your border.

18. Join in a white string and continue stitching, but double up on your stitching by criss-crossing each stitch. Keep double stitching until you've done half a row, then trim the bundle of grasses for a thinner end. Complete the top row and secure it with a couple of extra stitches to finish your two-toned bowl.

Flower pattern bowl

Combining three patterns and three distinctive colours, this coiled flower-patterned bowl is perfect to welcome spring, but is also fun to make all year-round.

Materials:

12m (13¼ yards) of your preferred
   core material, making a bundle 1.5cm
   (⅝ inch) in diameter
17 x 1-m (39-inch) lengths of red plastic string
17 x 1-m (39-inch) lengths of turquoise
   plastic string
6 x 1-m (39-inch) lengths of black plastic string
3 large-eyed needles
Ruler or measuring tape
Scissors

1. Gather 10–12 strands of your preferred dried material for the core of your basket, making a bundle 1.5cm (⅝ inch) in diameter, and 1 red plastic string for the stitching material. Begin a round base with 11 rows (see steps 1 and 2, page 24).

2. On row 12, begin alternating 25 red stitches with 2 turquoise stitches.

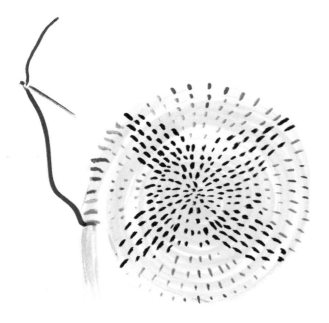

3. From row 13 to row 16, alternate red and turquoise stitches to create the flower pattern, while shaping the basket by placing rows directly on top of one another (see steps 5 and 6, page 26). Add extra turquoise stitches each time you reach the previous ones so they stay aligned. This will result in blocks of 4 turquoise stitches on row 13, 9 turquoise stitches on row 14, 18 turquoise stitches on row 15, and 32 turquoise stitches on row 16.

4. From row 17, add a third colour to create the reverse triangle that will act as a decorative border as you near the top edge of your bowl. Alternate 17 turquoise stitches, 7 red stitches, 17 turquoise stitches, 2 black stitches on row 17.

5. Alternate 15 turquoise stitches, 4 red stitches, 15 turquoise stitches and 4 black stitches on row 18.

6. Alternate 18 turquoise stitches, 2 red stitches, 18 turquoise stitches and 8 black stitches on row 19 to complete your flower pattern.

7. Continue to build your decorative triangle on row 20 with blocks of 12 black stitches and 16 black stitches.

8. On row 21, alternate blocks of 22 black stitches and 22 turquoise stitches.

9. On row 22, alternate blocks of 26 black stitches and 16 turquoise stitches.

10. Row 23 is the final top row, so double up on your stitches by criss-crossing each stitch. You need to do this all around the top edge of the bowl until you reach and finish the 4th and final black triangle. Once here, trim off any excess fibre and secure it with a couple of extra stitches.

Creating a basket wall

Basket walls are a continuation of the gallery-wall trend that has become increasingly popular in interior design over the past few years as a means of displaying family photos, art pieces and prints and creating a stunning focal point in any room.

The real beauty of a basket wall is that you can mix and match them – the more patterns and textures, the better. Here are some of my tips to create one of your own:

1. First find your wall! A basket wall works perfectly above a bed, sofa or fireplace, or in that awkward, narrow little corner in the hallway. If you want your bedroom to have a calm and relaxed vibe, make sure you opt for a softer colour palette or choose baskets made from natural cane and willow.

2. Plan your layout. Start by laying your selection of baskets on the floor and arrange and re-arrange them until you're happy with the layout. Make sure you create a focal point with an oversized piece, but that doesn't necessarily have to be positioned in the centre of your display.

3. Think outside the box. Don't have a big selection of baskets? Fear not – you can play around with different objects that will add dimension to your wall. Try mirrors, hats, masks, prints or art pieces.

4. Hang your baskets. You'll need nails or picture hooks and a hammer. You don't need to be super-precise or use a spirit level to make they are all straight. I use paper clips to hang the baskets created in this chapter as their bases are quite flat. Simply thread a paper clip through the stitching material and then hang it on the wall.

5. Don't be afraid to keep adding! Your basket wall is never really 'finished' – you may decide to add more baskets or swap some around. But if you change your mind and want a different display, all you need to do is lift the basket off the wall and put it back in the kitchen!

Flat lid storage basket

Keep clutter hidden away under the lid of this beautiful and minimalist storage basket. Cut-out handles on each side make it easy to open and move around. The design has been kept to a minimum so you can get used to weaving baskets in bigger sizes.

Materials:

For the basket
40m (43¾ yards) of your preferred core material, making a bundle 1.5cm (⅝ inch) in diameter
110 x 1-m (39-inch) lengths of white plastic string
Large-eyed needle
Measuring tape
Scissors

For the handles
Plastic-headed pins
Craft knife
10 x 1-m (39-inch) lengths of white plastic string

For the lid
16m (17½ yards) of your preferred core material, making a bundle 1.5cm (⅝ inch) in diameter
54 x 1-m (39-inch) lengths of white plastic string

Make sure you keep your stitches even –
as you build up the sides, any unevenness
will be magnified.

1. Gather 10–12 strands of your preferred dried material, making a bundle 1.5cm (⅝ inch) in diameter, for the core of your basket and 1 piece of plastic string for the stitching material. Begin a round base (see steps 1 and 2, page 24).

2. When you have worked 22 rows of stitching measuring 30cm (12 inches) in diameter and have a solid base, you can start to coil up the sides of the basket and shape the basket (see steps 5 and 6, page 26).

3. Continue working in a spiral, but start row 23 by placing coils directly on top of another. The stitches continue as before. Make sure you are holding the core material in the correct place and using each stitch to hold it there.

4. Continue building the sides and keep a close eye on the shape from different angles and on your tension for an even basket with straight sides. Join in new materials when necessary (see steps 3 and 4, page 25) and work the sides up for 40 rows, measuring approx 19cm (7½ inches) high.

5. Trim a few strands of the core material to make a thinner bundle and finish row 42 by wrapping the stitching material tightly into the core.

The handles

6. Place your basket on a flat surface. Mark a point on the 3rd row from the top with a pin – this is where your handle will start. Measure and insert a second pin 6cm (2¼ inches) along from the first pin.

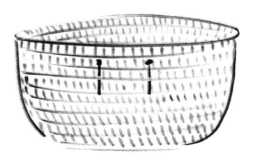

7. Measure down 2cm (¾ inch) from these two pins, and insert pins at these points. These pins mark the two rows to be removed for the rectangular hole for a handle.

8. Using a craft knife, carefully cut the inside of the rectangle. Repeat the process exactly opposite to make the second handle.

9. Use stitching material to strengthen the cut-out sides of your handles and to ensure the core material doesn't unravel. Double stitch each side with white string.

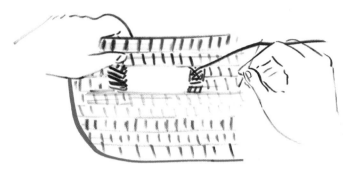

10. Your completed basket should measure approx 21cm (8¼ inches) high with a top diameter of 38cm (15 inches), with two cut-out handles of 6 x 2cm (2¼ x ¾ inch).

The lid

11. Make a flat base of 24 rows measuring 38cm (15 inches) in diameter (see steps 1 and 2, page 24). Lay the lid on the basket and check the diameter to make sure your lid will fit properly.

12. Working on the wrong side of the lid, start your next row by placing rows directly on top of another (see steps 5 and 6, page 26). This will make the rim of the lid which will sit outside the basket. Make a total of 3 rows.

13. Finish by trimming a few strands of core material to make a thinner bundle and wrap the stitching material tightly into the core.

Ali Baba basket

I grew up with the folk tale of *Ali Baba and the Forty Thieves* in which Ali Baba discovers that forty thieves have hidden a treasure in a cave. This is your very own Ali Baba basket, which can hide away a different type of treasure: toys, laundry and any other trinkets you have around the house. This is an ambitious project to tackle, but extremely gratifying when completed. The design is a repeat pattern and I would strongly encourage you to master the triangle pattern bowl on pages 46–49 before moving on to this project.

Materials:

For the basket
35m (38¼ yards) of your preferred core material, making a bundle 1.5cm (⅝ inch) in diameter
105 x 1-m (39-inch) lengths of white plastic string
30 x 1-m (39-inch) lengths of turquoise plastic string
2 large-eyed needles
Measuring tape
Scissors

For the handles
10 x 1-m (39-inch) lengths of white plastic string
10 x 1-m (39-inch) lengths of turquoise plastic string
Plastic-headed pins
Bodkin
Craft knife

For the lid
17m (15½ yards) of your preferred core material, making a bundle 1.5cm (⅝ inch) in diameter
54 x 1-m (39-inch) lengths of white plastic string
8 x 1-m (39-inch) lengths of turquoise plastic string

1. Gather 10–12 strands of your preferred dried material, making a bundle 1.5cm (⅝ inch) in diameter, for the core of your basket and one piece of white string for the stitching material. Begin a round base (see steps 1 and 2, page 24).

2. When you have worked 15 rows of stitching measuring 23cm (9 inches) in diameter and have a solid base, you can start to coil up the sides of the basket and shape the basket, starting row 16 by placing coils directly on top of another (see steps 5 and 6, page 26). The stitches continue as before. Make sure you are holding the core material in the correct place, using each stitch to hold it there.

3. Continue building the sides and keep a close eye on the shape from different angles and on your tension for an even basket with straight sides. Join in new materials when necessary (see steps 3 and 4, page 25) and work your sides up for another 4 rows.

4. From row 22 to row 28, alternate white and turquoise stitches to create the triangle pattern as seen in the photo, while shaping the basket by placing rows directly on top of another. Add extra turquoise stitches each time you reach the previous ones so they stay aligned. This will result in the following pattern:
Row 22: 45 white stitches, 2 turquoise stitches, 45 white stitches, 2 turquoise stitches, 45 white stitches.
Increase to 3 turquoise stitches on row 23, 4 turquoise stitches on row 24, 5 turquoise stitches on row 25, 6 turquoise stitches on row 26, 7 turquoise stitches on row 27, 8 turquoise stitches on row 28.
You have now completed the bottom row of three triangles.

5. The three triangles in the middle row will each be positioned in between the first three triangles. Start row 29 with a white string and do 25 stitches – your last stitch should be inbetween the last 2 rows of turquoise stitching on row 28. Join in a turquoise string and do 2 turquoise stitches that will act as the base for your 4th triangle. Continue alternating 25 white stitches and 2 turquoise stitches until you have completed a full row and have the bases of your next three triangles.

6. Then follow this pattern:
3 turquoise stitches on row 30, 4 turquoise stitches on row 31, 5 turquoise stitches on row 32, 6 turquoise stitches on row 33, 7 turquoise stitches on row 34, 8 turquoise stitches on row 35.
You have now completed the middle row of three triangles.

7. You are now going to create the top row of three triangles. These triangles need to line up with the bottom row so stitch in white for 50–52 stitches (depending on your tension), then add 2 turquoise stitches.

8. Work as in the previous steps until you have completed the base of the top row of three triangles, and then complete the triangles as before.

9. Once you've completed your 9th and final triangle, continue stitching with the white string, but double up the stitching by criss-crossing each stitch. Keep double-stitching until you reach the top of the final triangle. Once here, trim off any excess fibre and secure it with a couple of extra stitches.

The handles

10. Prepare all the materials you need for the handles and put 5 white strings and 5 turquoise strings aside.

11. Place your basket on a flat surface. Decide where the handle will start, making sure you pick a place where there's only white stitching so your handle doesn't cover the triangle pattern.

12. Mark a point between rows 2 and 3 with a plastic pin and mark a second point 5cm (2 inches) further along. Do the same on the direct opposite side of the basket for the second handle. As with the first handle, this should not cover the pattern, so adjust the position of both handles if necessary.

13. Using a bodkin or a craft knife, create a gap at the first pin and insert a bundle of 5 white and 5 turquoise strings on the inside of the basket. Tie them together with a knot on the inside of the basket.

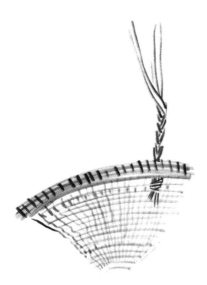

14. On the outside of the basket, make a 15-cm (6-inch) braid from the plastic strings. Using the bodkin or craft knife, create a gap at the second pin and insert the other end of the strings. Tie another knot on the inside so the handle is firmly secured. Leave a 1-cm (½-inch) tail after each knot and trim off any excess string.

15. Repeat to make a second handle on the other side of the basket.

See overleaf for how to make the lid >>

The lid

16. Using white string, make a flat base of 4 rows, measuring 5cm (2 inches) in diameter. Start to coil up the sides for 6 rows, keeping your stitching quite tight. This forms the handle on the top of the lid.

17. Then start stitching out again (your work should have a shape similar to a reversed funnel) for 8 rows.

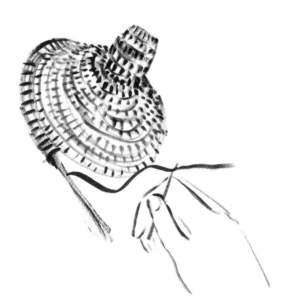

18. Following the same patten you have created for the basket, re-introduce the turquoise triangle pattern – start row 19 with 2 turquoise stitches, growing row by row to 9 turquoise stitches to complete three triangles.

19. Stitch one full row (row 27) of white stitches.

20. Revert to the triangle pattern on the following row (see step 4) and start creating the bases of three more triangles with 2 turquoise stitches on row 28 and 3 turquoise stitches on row 29.

21. Lay the lid on top of the basket and check that the external diameter of your lid is the same diameter as your basket. If not, continue stitching these three triangles until your lid fits properly on top of the basket.

22. Finish by trimming extra strands and double stitching.

23. To make the inner rim of your lid, measure the inner diameter of your basket and stitch 2 rows with white plastic strings of that length.

24. Attach the inner rim to the underside of the main lid by stitching both parts with white strings to finish.

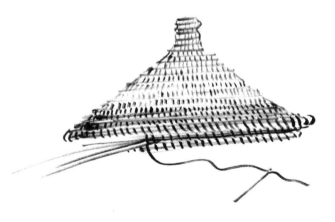

If your project starts to look or feel wobbly, don't hesitate to increase the number of stitches per row to stabilize it.

Adapting your project

Baskets come in all sizes, shapes and patterns and if you're feeling a bit adventurous and would like to adapt or personalize some of the projects in this book, here are a few things to bear in mind.

Size

The exact dimensions of any finished project will always depend on the materials used and how tightly or loosely you work. Each person works with a different tension and the majority of projects in this book allow for this by being generous with the materials you will require.

The difference in tightness can also lead to variations in the size of the finished project. Measure your piece as you work and if needed adjust your weaving, working tighter or a bit looser.

The base of your basket will always dictate how big or how small your basket will be, so be sure to keep an eye on it if you would like to create a bigger basket.

Design

The options are endless…

The easiest way to make a basket your own is to change the stitching colours, perhaps even just for a border. You don't have to make any other changes and yet this immediately personalizes your basket.

Some of my favourite patterns to create include squares, rectangles and zigzag lines. All geometrical shapes work brilliantly on the baskets and you simply have to increase or decrease the number of coloured stitches on every other row to achieve this look.

If you have a pattern in mind or are inspired by something you've seen, I would encourage you to roughly sketch it and decide on colours before starting to create.

Cane

Cane

With their natural creamy colours and beautiful woven patterns, cane baskets are one of the most instantly recognizable types of basket on the market. The centre cane used in basket weaving comes from the inside of the rattan palm, which grows wild in the jungles and virgin forests of tropical countries – the best cane grows in South-east Asia and Africa. Its outer skin is covered with hooked thorns that are stripped off before the cane is split into varying thicknesses – see the chart on the facing page for the sizes of cane I use in this book.

Centre cane is too brittle to be woven in its dry state, so you will need to soak it in lukewarm water to make it easier to manipulate. Soaking times depend on the thickness and should be stated on the packaging when you purchase it, but the general rule is if you can bend the cane without cracking it, it is ready to be used!

Working with cane is referred to as 'stake and strand' – first the flat base (or 'slath', see page 76) is woven with horizontal 'strands', then vertical 'stakes' are attached to that base to create the structure of the sides. Once the sides are woven, these stakes are then used to create the border at the top. See the step-by-step photos on pages 76–80 – these show the basic techniques used in all the projects. When looping a piece of cane around your slath to start weaving, you will end up with two weavers, one on either side of your stakes – these are generally referred to as the left-hand weaver and the right-hand weaver (although they will change sides as you work).

When working with cane, you'll need a bucket filled with water, trips to the sink to ensure the water stays lukewarm, and a lot of patience when cane won't bend. The answer is always to let it soak a little longer while you grab a cup of tea!

Centre cane conversion chart

This handy conversion chart will help you to choose the correct size of cane. Some suppliers describe the size in either millimetres or fractions of an inch; other suppliers describe the size by number – but please note that the numbering system is not the same in the UK and USA.

If you are unable to find the exact thickness specified in the project, don't hesitate to use the next size up (there are more sizes than listed here – these five sizes are the ones I have used in this book).

UK number	No. 5	No. 6	No. 8	No. 10	No. 14
Diameter (mm)	2.5mm	2.65mm	3mm	3.3mm	4.25mm
US number	No. 3	No. 4	No. 4.5	No. 5	No. 6.5
Diameter (inches)	3/32	7/64	1/8	9/64	3/16

Weaving technique

The pairing technique is used in all the projects in this section – you'll be weaving with two pieces of cane around the base of your basket. Simply weave your working piece of cane (A) in front of the stake to its right and over your second weaver (B).

The diagram below demonstrates this technique in action from the side. It is important that one weaver does not overtake the other at any point. Also read the following pages for more tips on the pairing technique.

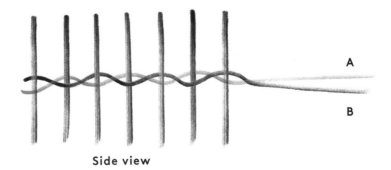

Side view

Cane how to

This section guides you through some of the basics to create a stake and strand basket using centre cane, including how to weave a base, join in new stakes, and shape and create a border. This technique forms the basis of all the cane projects.

1. Making a slath is the starting point for all cane baskets. Using cane cutters, cut 8 20-cm (8-inch) lengths of centre cane in the size specified in the project. To make a 4-through-4 slath using your bodkin, gather the stakes into 2 groups of 4. Start by piercing one of the stakes in the middle with your bodkin.

2. Repeat with your next 3 stakes, so you have 4 pierced stakes in total.

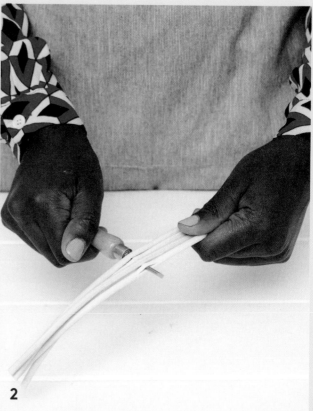

3. Poke the remaining 4 unpierced stakes through the 4 pierced ones to form a cross. (Some projects in this chapter require a 3-through-3 slath or a 6-through-6 slath – these are made in the same way.) Once you've completed your slath, start soaking a couple of lengths of cane in lukewarm water (loop each length of cane into a bundle and tie it so that it fits into your bucket and doesn't unravel in the water).

4. Loop one cane (the weaver) around 4 of the stakes and pull it down to sit next to the crossed pieces. Hold the weaver on the bottom (A) with your left thumb (this is the piece diagonally crossing the centre in the photo) and take the weaver on the top (B) in front of the first group of 4 stakes and behind the next group of 4 stakes. Pull tightly, then rotate the slath a quarter turn anti-clockwise. A is now on top, and B is underneath. Hold B in place with your left thumb, and take A in front of the next group of 4 stakes and behind the next group of 4 stakes. Pull tightly, then rotate the slath a quarter anti-clockwise. A is now underneath, and B is on top. Repeat until you have completed 2 rows.

3

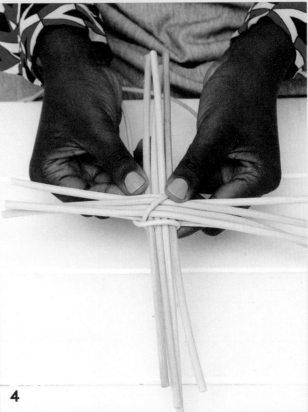

4

5. Next, separate the stakes into groups of 2 using the same pairing weave. Hold the weaver on the bottom (A) with your left thumb and take the weaver on the top (B) in front of the next 2 stakes and behind the next group of 2 stakes. Pull tightly, then rotate the slath a quarter turn anti-clockwise. A is now on top, and B is underneath.

6. Repeat the pairing sequence in step 5 until you have completed 3 rows and increased the size of the base.

5

6

7. Before opening the stakes to singles, pull the stakes apart a little so that the weaving can go down into the spaces between the stakes to ensure the weaving stays tight. Don't hesitate to re-soak your cane if it doesn't feel flexible enough. Try to keep the stakes open evenly.

8. When the base has reached the desired size, start shaping the sides of the basket by adding new stakes that will be turned up vertically. Cut new stakes with your cutters and insert them on the right side of your base stakes, using the bodkin to create some space. Let it soak for a few minutes, then using pliers, pinch each stake at the base and bend it upwards.

9. The projects in this book use a simple decorative border. Once your basket has reached the desired height, soak the stakes in lukewarm water for 5–10 minutes. Using pliers, pinch each stake at the base to fold it to the right.

10. Select one stake and pull it behind the stake to its right and out to the front of the basket. Then take the stake you just went behind and bring it behind the stake to its right and then to the front of the basket. Continue to weave each stake to the front in this manner until you have completed a full row. Finally, trim the ends evenly, but do not cut them too short or the rim will come undone.

9

10

Always make sure any excess centre cane from a project is left to dry out, as damp cane will go mouldy if stored in a bag or a box!

Breakfast tray

The first time I posted a picture of this cane tray on social media, someone commented that the 'process looks both relaxing and satisfying' and I couldn't have said it better myself.

This is one of my favourite projects to make and it really showcases the natural cane. It's also ideal for a beginner. Once you've perfected the technique, feel free to play around with dyed cane (see page 91) and use different colours to enhance the weaving.

Materials:
Centre cane:
　3.3mm ($\frac{9}{64}$ inch) for the stakes
　2.5mm ($\frac{3}{32}$ inch) for the weavers
　(see the chart on page 75 regarding cane sizes)
Cane cutters
Bodkin
Pliers
Measuring tape
Bucket of lukewarm water, plus a towel

1. Prepare all your materials and make sure you work on a flat surface. Cut 8 x 20-cm (8-inch) lengths of 3.3mm (9/64 inch) cane.

2. Make a 4-through-4 slath by piercing 4 of the stakes with the bodkin and poke the other 4 stakes through the pierced ones to form a cross (see steps 1–3, pages 76–77).

3. Put your slath and a couple of bundles of the 2.5mm (3/32 inch) cane in a bucket of lukewarm water to soak for 5 minutes or so.

4. You are now going to start weaving the base using one length of soaked 2.5mm (3/32 inch) cane and tying it with 2 rows of pairing. Make sure you pull on the weavers firmly (see steps 4–5, pages 77–78).

5. On row 3, open the stakes to groups of 2 and on row 5 open them to singles, ensuring that the space between each stake is even (see steps 6–7, pages 78–79).

6. Now that all your stakes are open to singles, weave another 6 rows, joining in new weavers when necessary and soaking in the base and weavers when the cane feels dry and more difficult to manipulate.

7. Continue weaving with rows of pairing and keep the base flat using a book, a weight or anything else heavy you have to hand.

8. Cut the weaver ends with your cutters very carefully, making sure the ends rest against the pattern and follow the weaving pattern.

9. Cut 16 x 50-cm (20-inch) stakes from the 3.3mm (9/64 inch) cane and insert one to the right of the base stakes using your bodkin as far as it will go (see step 8, page 79). Repeat until all 16 stakes have been inserted.

10. To give the tray a gentle curve, push the stakes away from you for another 4–5 rows of pairing.

11. Complete the weaving once you've reached 35 rows and the tray is 45cm (18 inches) across.

12. Now make the border. Soak the stakes for 5–10 minutes in lukewarm water, then pinch them at the base using your pliers ahead of getting your border started (see step 9, page 80).

13. Pick one of the stakes and thread it through the upright stake (see step 10, page 80). Repeat until all stakes have been threaded through and trim the excess at the back of your basket.

Dyed basket

One of my favourite places back in Senegal is Le Lac Rose – it's a beautiful and scenic lake with pink water! It has different shades of pink depending on the season and time of the day, and this magical place was my inspiration for weaving this bowl. The result is a combination of fuchsia pink, rosy pink and baby pink, all obtained by dyeing cane for different amounts of time.

Materials:
Pink fabric dye
Centre cane:
   3mm (⅛ inch) for the stakes
   2.65mm (⁷⁄₆₄ inch) for the weavers
   (see the chart on page 75 regarding cane sizes)
Cane cutters
Pliers
Bodkin
Measuring tape
Piece of ribbon or twine
Bucket of lukewarm water, plus a towel

Avoid putting your cane baskets in a hot room or next to heaters, as the humidity will dry out the cane and make them brittle.

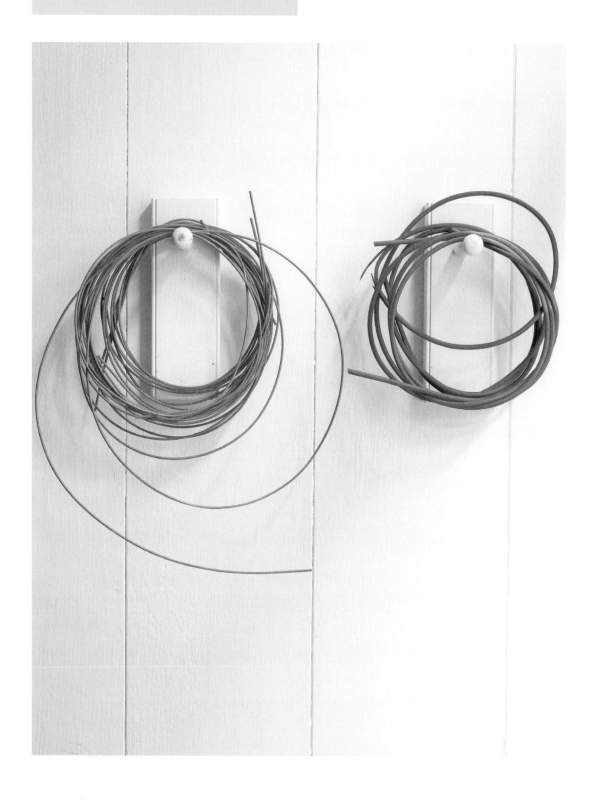

1. Dye 12–15 bundles of 2.65mm (⁷⁄₆₄ inch) cane (see page 91). I've used just one shade of pink, but let the cane soak for different times to get varying hues of pink.

2. Cut 12 x 60-cm (24-inch) lengths of cane from your bundle of 3mm (⅛ inch) cane and make a 6-through-6 slath (see steps 1–3, pages 76–77).

3. Let your 6-through-6 slath and 2 bundles of pink-dyed cane soak in lukewarm water for 5 minutes.

4. Start your base by weaving 2 rows of pairing with 1 length of pink-dyed cane (see steps 4–5, pages 77–78).

5. When you next join in a new weaver, start playing with colours and use a bundle of cane in a lighter or darker shade of pink. Continue to repeat this process throughout the rest of the work.

6. On row 3, open the stakes to groups of 3 and on row 5, open them out to singles for 2 more rows (see steps 6–7, pages 78–79).

7. Start pushing the stakes away from you to create the curved sides of the baskets and use ribbon or twine to tie them all together.

8. You are now working the sides. Continue weaving and shaping the basket until it reaches a height of 11cm (4½ inches) and don't forget to alternate different shades of pink when joining in a new weaver.

9. When your basket measures 11cm (4½ inches) high and 20cm (8 inches) across, trim off your 2 weavers and insert 2 new weavers in the same colour to create a pre-border in one solid colour (this will really contrast with what you've woven so far).

10. Weave 8 more rows.

11. Trim the weavers and to ensure they do not unravel, make sure each weaver lays against a stake.

12. Trim the stakes so you have 20cm (8 inches) of unwoven cane, soak them for 10 minutes, pinch them and start weaving your decorative border (see steps 9–10, page 80).

13. Trim the stakes on the inside of the basket using your cutters.

Dyeing cane

Baskets used to be coloured with natural materials, such as onion skins or cochineal, and although these materials can still be used today, fabric dyes offer an easy, quick and cost-effective way to bring colour to a project. Follow the packet instructions, plus my tips below.

1. Always work in a well-ventilated room and wear rubber gloves to prevent your hands from getting stained.

2. Tie your centre cane into small bundles that will easily fit into the dye solution.

3. To enhance the colour, you can add one cup of salt to the dye solution.

4. Depending on the manufacturer's instructions and the shade you would like to achieve, your bundles can remain in the dye solution from 10 minutes up to 1 hour – don't forget to stir the mixture to ensure even dyeing.

5. Always rinse your dyed cane in cool water, then hang it up to dry before you start to weave it.

Cane care

The number one rule to follow when working with cane is DO NOT OVERSOAK IT! Soaking cane for too long weakens the fibres and make them prone to snapping.

When purchasing centre cane either online or in store, you will always get an indication of soaking time depending on the thickness you buy – keep this number in mind when weaving your basket!

It is quite handy to spritz the cane with a water spray if it starts to dry out or you can also wrap your bundles in a damp towel so they don't dry out too quickly.

If you have soaked cane leftover when you have finished a project, allow it to dry out before storing it as this will prevent it going mouldy.

Lampshade

A good lampshade can make or break a space – fact! I love how this woven cane shade creates an interesting play of light and shadow on the ceiling of a living room, bedroom or corridor.

This project will continue to help you refine your stake-and-strand technique and perfect your shaping.

Materials:
Centre cane:
   3.3mm ($^9/_{64}$ inch) for the stakes
   2.65mm ($^7/_{64}$ inch) for the weavers
   (see the chart on page 75 regarding
   cane sizes)
Cane cutters
Bodkin
Pliers
Measuring tape
Bucket of lukewarm water,
  plus a towel
Lampholder and electrical flex

If you wish, give the lampshade (or any cane project) a coat of acrylic varnish to enhance the colour and provide a protective layer.

1. Cut 8 x 10-cm (4-inch) lengths from the 3.3mm (⁹⁄₆₄ inch) cane bundle and make a 4-through-4 slath using your bodkin (see steps 1–3, pages 76–77).

2. Soak your slath and a couple of bundles of 2.65mm (⁷⁄₆₄ inch) cane in lukewarm water until the slath and bundles begin to feel more pliable.

3. Start weaving the base using the freshly soaked 2.65mm (⁷⁄₆₄ inch) cane and tying it firmly with 3 rows of pairing (see steps 4–5, pages 77–78).

4. On row 4, open the stakes to groups of 2 for 3 rows (see step 6, page 78).

5. On row 7, open the stakes to singles for 3 rows, making sure the space between each stake is even (see step 7, page 79). Your base is now complete and should measure 6cm (2¼ inches) across.

6. Cut 16 x 35-cm (14-inch) lengths of 3.3mm (⁹⁄₆₄ inch) cane. Using your bodkin, insert each one to the right of each stake (see step 8, page 79).

7. Soak the stakes for 5 minutes in lukewarm water. Using the pliers, bend them at the base so you can start shaping the basket.

8. Continue pairing using freshly soaked 2.65mm (⁷⁄₆₄ inch) cane and shaping the basket. Stop at the end of a row to look at your work from different angles and make sure the shape is coming along nicely. If you need to reshape the basket, soak it for a few minutes and reshape it by holding firmly with both of your hands.

9. Continue weaving until your lampshade is about 25cm (10 inches) high and the diameter is about 30cm (12 inches).

10. You should have 15cm (6 inches) of unwoven cane from each stake – soak these 16 stakes in lukewarm water for 5–10 minutes. Use your pliers to bend each stake sideways.

11. To make the border, thread each stake through the stake on its right, and repeat until all stakes have been threaded through (see steps 9–10, page 80). Trim any excess that doesn't lay against the basket.

See overleaf for how to finish the lampshade >>

12. To insert the lampholder into the lampshade, carefully cut through the centre of your 4-through-4 slath with your cutters. The size of the hole will vary depending on the size of your fitting so make sure you measure it before making your hole.

14. Once you are all set up and your fitting is attached, light it up and bask in its glow.

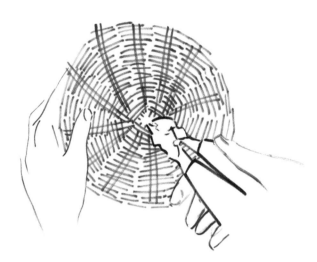

13. If you feel confident and have experience of adding the light fitting yourself, the next step is to set up your light. Otherwise please seek the help of a professional as fittings and laws differ from country to country.

Birkin bag

Summer is one of my favourite seasons and I love seeing women rocking a basket bag during the warmer months. This little number is inspired by the iconic Jane Birkin and is the perfect accessory for balmy evenings near the beach or for a stroll with friends in the city. You can adapt the size if you wish, and why not line the inside of the basket with fabric to give it a personal look?

Materials:
Centre cane:
   3.3mm (⁹⁄₆₄ inch) for the stakes
   2.65mm (⁷⁄₆₄ inch) for the weavers
   2.5mm (³⁄₃₂ inch) for the handle
   (see the chart on page 75 regarding cane sizes)
Cane cutters
Bodkin
Pliers
Measuring tape
Bucket of lukewarm water, plus a towel
Piece of ribbon or twine, or an elastic band
Weight

1. Cut 6 x 15-cm (6-inch) lengths of 3.3mm (⁹⁄₆₄ inch) cane and make a 3-through-3 slath (see steps 1–3, pages 76–77). Soak your slath and a couple of bundles of 2.65mm (⁷⁄₆₄ inch) cane in lukewarm water.

2. Start weaving your base tightly with 3 rows of pairing using the freshly soaked 2.5mm (³⁄₃₂ inch) cane (see steps 4–6, pages 77–78).

3. Open the stakes to singles on row 4 and continue weaving until you've done 8 rows (see step 7, page 79).

4. Stake up with 12 pieces of 30-cm (12-inch) cane cut from the 3.3mm (⁹⁄₆₄ inch) bundle of cane and bend them up at the base with the pliers so you can start shaping the basket (see step 8, page 79).

5. Tie your stakes tightly together with a piece of ribbon or twine so you can start weaving the sides. Make sure you work from a flat surface, using a weight to keep your base flat.

6. Continue weaving with rows of pairing using freshly-soaked 2.5mm (³⁄₃₂ inch) cane until the basket is about 25cm (10 inches) high and 18cm (7 inches) across.

7. Soak and pinch the stakes before threading them through to create a simple decorative border (see steps 9–10, page 80).

See overleaf for how to create the handle >>

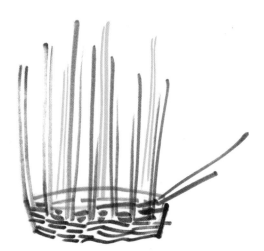

The handle

8. To create the handle, you will require a slim bundle 80cm (31½ inches) long of 3.3mm (⁹⁄₆₄ inch) cane. Insert this handle on opposite side of the basket, pushing the end in as far as possible. The external handle should be about 40cm (16 inches).

9. Cut 4 x 1-m (39-inch) lengths of 2.5mm (³⁄₃₂ inch) cane. Use the bodkin to thread them to the left of the handle, then let them soak for 10 minutes.

10. Working clockwise, start wrapping the 4 lengths around the handle until you've reached the other side of the handle.

11. Wrap anti-clockwise from the right side of the handle to the left side and finally wrap clockwise from the left side of the handle to the right side.

12. Using the bodkin, thread the remaining cane – you should have about 10cm (4 inches) – through the basket. Trim off any excess cane.

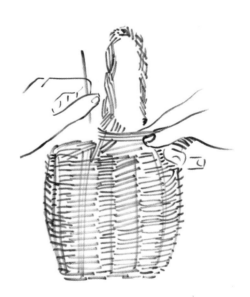

Picnic basket

Living in London, I'm spoiled with outdoor spaces and beautiful gardens, so a picnic is always on the cards when the sun is shining. For my next outing, I wanted to give the traditional picnic basket a makeover by adding a scalloped edge to bring a touch of femininity and curves. This basket would also work perfectly for Easter filled with eggs and chocolates!

Materials:

Centre cane:
    4.25mm (³⁄₁₆ inch) for the stakes
    2.65mm (⁷⁄₆₄ inch) for the weavers
    (see the chart on page 75 regarding cane sizes)
Cane cutters
Bodkin
Pliers
Measuring tape
Piece of ribbon or twine, or an elastic band
Bucket of lukewarm water, plus a towel

1. Start by cutting 9 x 15-cm (6-inch) lengths of 4.25mm (³⁄₁₆ inch) cane and make a 4-through-4 slath (see steps 1–3, pages 76–77).

2. Soak your slath and a couple of bundles of 2.65mm (⁷⁄₆₄ inch) cane in lukewarm water.

3. Start your base by weaving 3 rows of pairing using the soaked 2.65mm (⁷⁄₆₄ inch) cane (see steps 4–5, pages 77–78).

4. On row 4, open the stakes into pairs (see step 6, page 78). Continue weaving as pairs until row 15 – your base should now measure about 18cm (7 inches) across.

5. Cut 16 x 50-cm (20-inch) lengths of 4.25mm (³⁄₁₆ inch) cane and stake up the base, 2 stakes to the right of each base stake (see step 8, page 79).

6. Start pushing the new stakes away from you to create the curved sides of the basket. Tie them all together with a length of twine so you can work the sides of your basket.

7. Continue weaving as the sides of your basket start to take shape. Make sure you control the overall shape by stopping and looking at your work from different angles. Don't forget to keep the base flat – use a stone, small bowl, heavy book or anything else in your kitchen with a good weight.

8. The sides of your baskets are completed once they reach 25cm (10 inches) high and 38cm (15 inches) across (you'll finish the top border after you have fitted the handle).

The scalloped edge

9. Finally, soak the stakes and thread each one to the left of its upright stake, creating a scalloped top border. Repeat until all are threaded, then trim off any excess.

The handle

10. To create the handle, soak 2 x 1-m (39-inch) lengths of 4.25mm (³⁄₁₆ inch) cane and insert them from one side to another to the right of the stakes.

11. Cut 6 x 80-cm (31½-inch) lengths of 2.65mm (⁷⁄₆₄ inch) cane. Wrap 3 times along the long handle before threading through the end.

Rope

Rope

All rope is not created equal! The market is currently split between synthetic ropes, such as nylon and polyester, and vegetable fibre ropes, such as cotton and hemp. Working with vegetable fibres is always my preference – they are spun from plants, are softer, more pliable and have been associated with weaving, macramé and other similar crafts for decades.

The principal vegetable fibres are manila, hemp, coir, cotton, sisal and jute (there's more on sisal and jute in the *Twine* chapter on page 122).

Manila is made from abaca leaves, a plant that belongs to the banana family and is highly praised for its elasticity and strength.

Hemp is cultivated in many parts of the world and has been used for centuries to make rope, canvas and paper.

Coir is extracted from the husk of coconuts and forms a particularly durable, water-resistant cordage.

Cotton needs no introduction as we are all familiar with it!

These fibres are twisted (twined) together to form ropes of two, three, four strands or are braided together. It is very difficult to sew through some of these ropes without breaking a needle or two, but cotton rope is a good all-round option that's suitable for all basket-making projects. You will need to use a sewing machine to give your basket the perfect finish!

When working with a twined rope, the strands are more likely to unravel under the needle if you don't catch both ropes in each stitch so I prefer using braided cotton which is accessible, cost-effective and easy to dye.

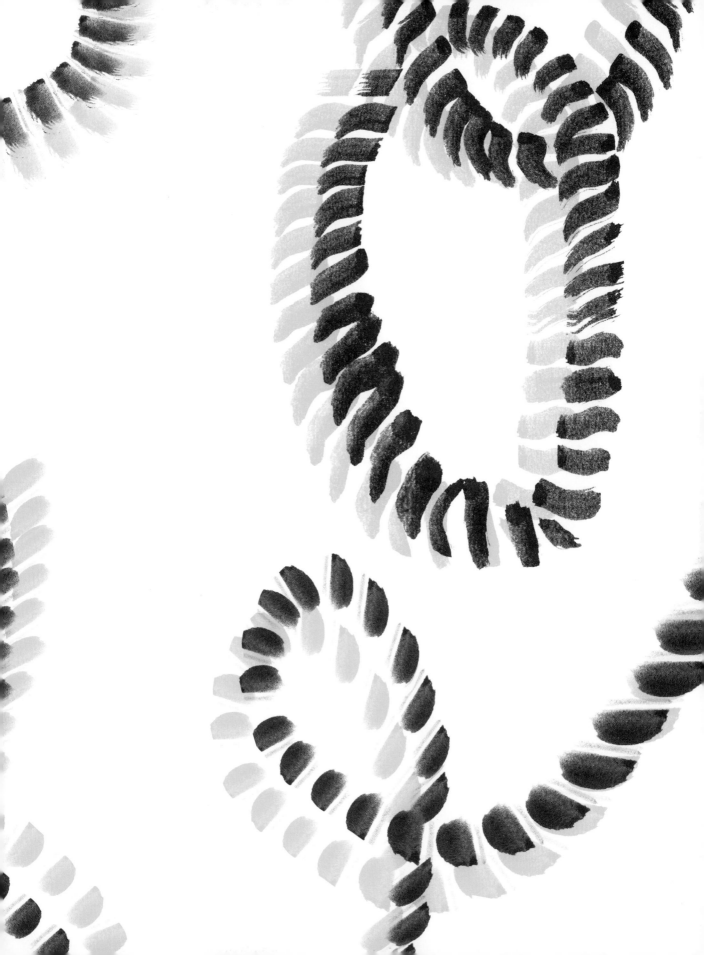

Rope how to

This section will guide you through some of the basic techniques needed to create a rope basket using cotton rope and your sewing machine, including how to make the base, zigzag stitch rope together, finish your basket and personalize it. Remember to thread your machine with extra-strong thread and to use a needle suitable for sewing jeans or leather.

1. Set your sewing machine to zigzag stitch. Untangle the rope and coil it in your hand into a circle measuring 2–2.5cm (¾–1 inch) in diameter. Secure it with a coloured pin (using a coloured pin makes it easier to see).

2. Place the coil under the foot of the sewing machine. Start stitching the rope together to secure the coil by zigzagging back and forth and catching the rope to either side. Continue stitching until your basket base is your desired size.

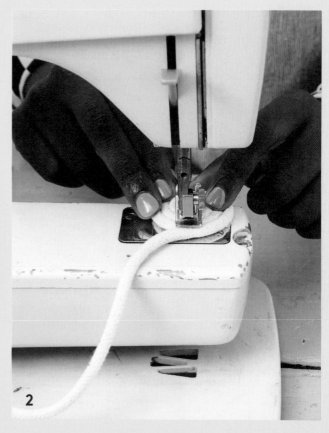

3. To start building the sides of the basket, angle the base against the left side of the machine and continue to sew as the side of your basket takes shape.

4. Continue to sew, gradually building up the rows of rope and making sure the zigzag stitch is catching both ropes in each stitch.

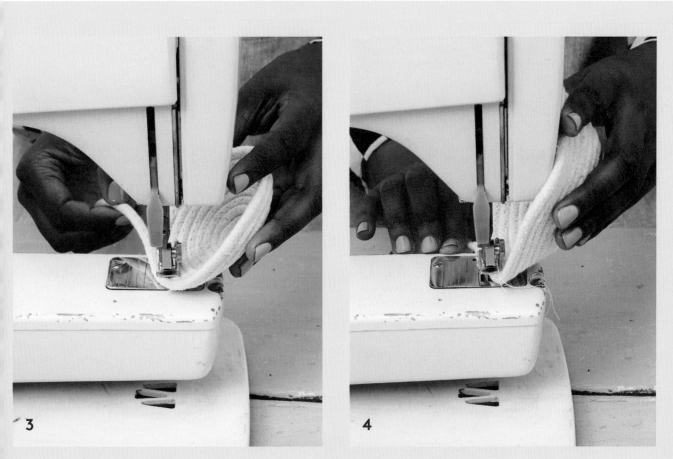

5. If you get to the end of your piece of rope and need to start a new length, simply place the pieces end to end and zigzag stitch them together.

6. When you've reached your desired height, loop the last few centimetres (inches) of rope back underneath itself so that the raw end is enclosed.

5

6

There are so many ways
to personalize your basket –
I especially like making fun fluffy
pompoms to sew onto the front.

Rope basket

A rope basket is a delight to make as cotton rope is soft, stretchy and extremely comfortable to use. Once you've perfected the technique, this basket can easily be in smaller or larger sizes, so why not make a matching set?

Materials:
15m (16½ yards) of 6-mm
   (¼-inch) cotton rope
Sewing machine with zigzag stitch, fitted
   with a needle for sewing jeans or leather
White extra-strong thread
Scissors
Ruler or measuring tape
Scissors
Sewing needle

1. Set your sewing machine to zigzag stitch and untangle the rope.

2. Coil the rope in your hand into a circle measuring 2–2.5cm (¾–1 inch) in diameter (see step 1, page 110) and place it under the needle.

3. Start stitching the rope together to secure the coil by zigzagging back and forth and catching the rope to either side (see step 2, page 110).

4. Your coil is now secured, so continue to zigzag stitch your base until it measures 12cm (4¾ inches) in diameter.

5. You are now ready to build the sides by angling the base against the left side of the sewing machine (see step 3, page 111).

6. Continue stitching as the sides of your bowl take shape.

7. Once the sides have reached about 15cm (6 inches) in height, finish your basket by looping under the last 3–5cm (1¼–2 inches) of loose rope (see steps 5–6, page 112).

Rope bag

Some bags will never go out of fashion, and a rope basket bag is exactly that! It's casual while being stylish, has enough room for all your day-to-day essentials and is an absolute pleasure to make. This bag consists of two identical halves which are then joined together.

Materials:

25m (27½ yards) of 8-mm (⅜-inch) cotton rope
Sewing machine with zigzag stitch, fitted with
   a needle for sewing jeans or leather
White extra-strong thread
Scissors
Ruler or measuring tape
Scissors
Pins

Tip:

This white cotton rope is washable, so if your bag becomes dirty, hand-wash it in cool water using a mild detergent.

1. Set your sewing machine to zigzag stitch. Coil the rope in your hand into a circle 2–2.5cm (¾–1 inch) in diameter (see step 1, page 110) and place it under the needle.

2. Start stitching to secure the coil, zigzagging back and forth and catching the rope to either side (see step 2, page 110).

3. Your coil is now secured, so continue to zigzag stitch your base until it measures around 33cm (13 inches) across.

4. Remove the stitched coil from the sewing machine but do not cut the rope. Fold your coil in half and measure 11cm (4⅜ inches) from the fold. Mark this point with a pin on each half. This is where your handle will start and end. Open the coil out flat again.

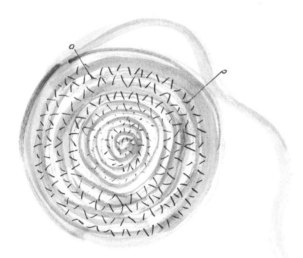

5. Replace the coil under the sewing machine needle and continue stitching another row in place until you reach the first pin. Measure out 24cm (9½ inches) of rope for your handle.

6. Replace the coil under the sewing machine needle at the second pin, leaving the handle loop of coil hanging loose. Continue sewing until you're back to the first pin.

7. To build up the handle, stitch a row of rope to the loose handle loop, then continue around the coil as usual. Repeat this so that the handle is 3 rows wide.

8. To stitch the sides of the bag, loop the rope back on itself and start sewing in the opposite direction all around the coil until you reach the other end of the handle. Repeat this until you have 4 rows extending beyond the handles. You have now completed the first side of your bag.

9. Repeat steps 1–8 to create the second side of your bag with the handle.

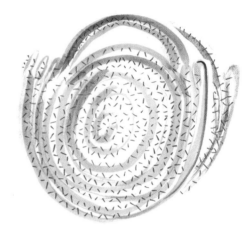

10. Hand sew the two sides together, making sure that the handles line up.

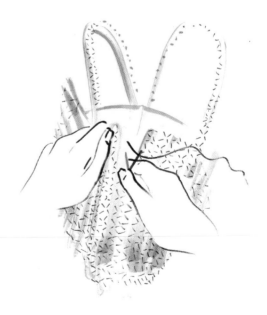

A great way to personalize this bag
would be to add leather to the handles to
reinforce them and add an elegant finish.

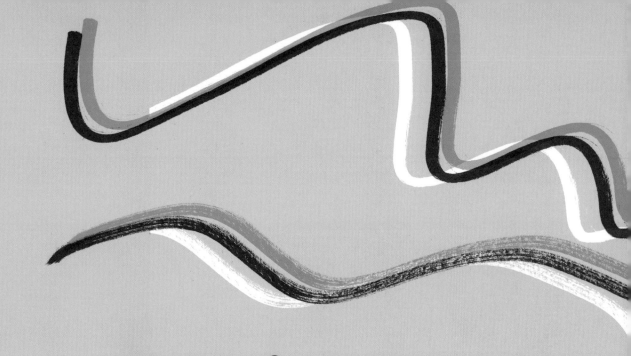

Twine

Twine

Sisal and jute are vegetable fibres and are my favourite materials to work with. Both materials are small enough to be carried in a handbag and you don't require much space or many tools – just pack a pair of scissors, a needle and a couple of rolls of jute twine and you can easily weave on a long car or train journey.

Working with these two fibres is often referred as 'twining'. Twining is believed to be older than weaving and consists of crossing the same pair of wefts (here the jute) over each wrap (here the sisal). There's a beautiful rhythm in twining and it provides a great sense of relaxation, much like knitting.

These days, sisal twine is often found in carpets, wall coverings or as part of a cat's scratching post! Extracted from the corchorus plant, it's coarse, strong and durable.

Jute is extracted from the jute plant and is considered to be one of the strongest vegetable fibres – it ranks second only to cotton in terms of the scale of its production. However, it is more environmentally friendly than cotton, which means it is used in countless products such as sacks, rugs and those hessian bags you've picked up at the supermarket to replace plastic options!

Jute twine has a very rustic feel in its natural colour of brown-beige. However, it takes dyes quite well and is often sold ready-dyed in an array of colours, making it really fun to personalize your projects.

Like most vegetable fibres, because these materials are used dry, they are easy to untangle or undo if you've made a mistake or want to restart your basket.

Twine how to

This section will guide you through some of the basics of twining with sisal twine and jute twine, including how to start your basket, shape it, add new colours and finish it.

1. Cut 8 x 30-cm (12-inch) lengths of sisal twine (the cream twine in the photo – these are the stakes). Cut a 3-m (3¼-yard) length of jute twine (the pink twine in the photo – this is the weaver). Line up the 8 lengths of sisal next to each other. Wrap the jute twine twice around the sisal twine, then tie a knot underneath so you have 2 equal lengths of jute at the front (these will be the left-hand and the right-hand weavers) and a knot at the back.

2. Split the sisal into 4 groups of 4, 2 groups below the knot and 2 above. Take the right weaver (A) from the back to the front by bringing it between the first and second group (above the knot) and hold down A with your left thumb so it sits with the fourth group below the knot.
2a. Take the left weaver (B) over the first group of 4 and under the second group. Rotate a quarter turn anti-clockwise.
2b. Release A and hold down B with your left thumb. Bring A over the second group

1

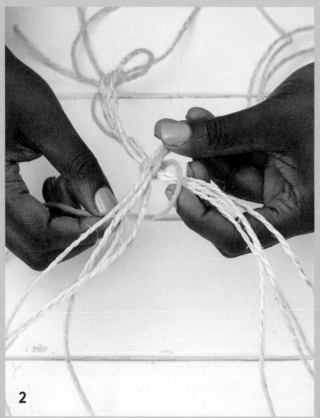

2

and under the third group. Rotate a quarter turn anti-clockwise.

2c. Release B and hold down A with your left thumb. Bring B over the third group and under the fourth group. Rotate a quarter turn anti-clockwise.

2d. Release A and hold down B with your left thumb. Bring A over the fourth group and under the first group. Rotate a quarter turn anti-clockwise.

2e. Release B and hold down A with your left thumb. You've now completed one row in the pairing sequence. Repeat the process until you have completed 3 full rows of pairing, always taking the weaver over the next stake to its right and under the one after.

3. Open your stakes to 2 by dividing the 4 groups of 4 into 8 groups of 2. Weave for 3 rows, then divide the groups of 2 into singles and weave in the same way for 3 rows. Remember to split groups by weaving between them from behind.

4. Continue the weaving until your base is the desired size. Always follow instructions, but as jute is a soft material (unlike cane), the rows can squashed down so don't worry if you do more or less rows. For a sturdier basket, add more stakes in the same way as for a cane basket (see step 8, page 79) – tie a knot at one end of a piece of sisal twine, place next to a stake so the knot is on the inside and weave them as pairs (don't open them to singles for 3–4 rows).

3

4

5. Start shaping your basket by tying all your stakes together with a piece of ribbon or an elastic band. You can use a little weight that would fit in your basket to hold it down while you weave the sides. Pull your weavers tightly enough to help hold the shape, but not so tightly that your basket becomes too narrow.

6. If you're nearing the end of a weaver (or want to change colour), make sure you have at least 5cm (2 inches) left and thread your weaver on to a needle. Move that weaver behind the stake as if you were going to weave it with it, but thread it through on the inside of the basket. Join in a new weaver where your left-hand weaver would have been coming out at the front, threading your new weaver in a new needle and thread it from the bottom to the top. Tie a knot on the inside of the basket to secure it.

5

6

7. Continue weaving until your basket has reached the desired height, making sure you have 5cm (2 inches) of your stakes left bare. Trim any loose ends as you go – the taller your basket becomes, the more difficult it will be to cut any excess twine close to the basket base.

8. To finish the top rim of your basket, thread the stakes onto a large-eyed needle and thread them down on the inside of your basket. Trim any loose ends.

Plant hanger

Forget boring brown and terracotta plant pots – a twine plant hanger makes an instant statement and gives our green friends the upgrade they deserve. Green and yellow, pink and blue, orange and red – the colour combinations are endless.

Materials:

For the basket
2m (2¼ yards) of sisal twine*
30m (33 yards) of turquoise jute twine*
3m (3¼ yards) of pink jute twine*
Large-eyed needle
Scissors
Measuring tape
Plastic plant pot*

For the basket hanger
Wooden ring
'S' hook
13m (14¼ yards) of pink jute twine
2m (2 yards) of turquoise jute twine

* Based on using a plastic plant pot
15cm (6 inches) high x 15cm (6 inches)
in diameter.

Succulents are the perfect plants for this project as they don't need to be watered too often and you can mist them with a spray bottle!

The basket

1. Cut 8 x 25-cm (10-inch) lengths of sisal twine. Tie a 3-m (3¼-yard) length of turquoise twine around the centre of the 8 pieces of sisal (see step 1, page 126).

2. Open into groups of 4 and weave 3 rows. On row 4 open to doubles and on row 7 open to singles (see steps 2–4, pages 126–127). Continue weaving until the diameter reaches 8cm (3¼ inches) – this is the base of your basket.

3. You are now going to start shaping the basket using the plant pot as a mould to get you started (see step 5, page 128). Weave 20 rows of pairing with the turquoise twine.

4. Thread the ends of the turquoise twine through and trim off any large excess before changing the colour.

5. Cut the pink twine into 2 x 1.5-m (1⅔ yards) lengths and join them in as your 2 new weavers (see step 6, page 128).

6. Weave 2 rows of pairing in pink, creating the coloured band, and thread the ends through.

7. Join in 2 x 3-m (3¼-yard) lengths of turquoise twine as your 2 new weavers and continue weaving in turquoise for about 30 rows. Once you've reached a height of 15cm (6 inches), your basket is complete.

8. Thread the stakes on the inside of the basket (see step 8, page 129). Tidy the inside of the basket by cutting any excess materials.

The macramé hanger

9. Cut 8 x 160-cm (1¾-yard) lengths of pink twine. Tie them together in pairs with a knot at each end.

10. Gather the 4 paired lengths of twine, fold them in the middle and push the looped centre through the wooden ring. Fold the tail ends under the ring and through the hooped centre of the twine and tug down firmly to secure the twine to the ring.

11. Hang the ring on an 'S' hook at a comfortable work height. Separate the 8 lengths of twine and pair them up. Measure 30cm (12 inches) down the twine and tie each pair with a square knot.

How to make a square knot (SK)
1. Start with 2 pairs on either side (A and B) and 2 pairs in the middle (the filler twines).
2. Pass B to the left, over the filler twines and behind A. Then take A to the right under the filler twines and up through the loop formed by B.
3. Then take A to the left, under the filler twines and over B. Take B to the right over the filler twines and down through the loop formed by A.
4. Pull on A and B equally tightly to secure.

A   B

12. Now separate the two pieces of twine at the bottom of each knot and partner them with a piece from the neighbouring knot and tie them together with a square knot a further 15cm (6 inches) down.

13. Now gather the 8 pieces of twine and tie them together in a crown knot (see below) 10cm (4 inches) down, using turquoise twine and ensuring it is tight.

How to make a crown knot (CK)
1. Gather your ends of twine into your fist and lay them out into a cross so none of the strands are touching.
2. Take strand A, lay loosely over strand B creating a loop.
3. Then take strand B over A and loosely lay over C, creating a loop.
4. Take strand C over B and loosely lay over D, creating a loop.
5. Take strand D and lay over C and under the loop created by A.
6. Gather up and pull tightly to secure your knot.

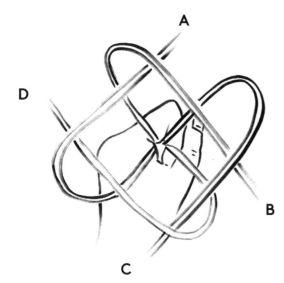

14. Once you have made up your macramé hanger, carefully place your chosen plant into your pot cover, and then place your pot into the hanger while it is hanging in position.

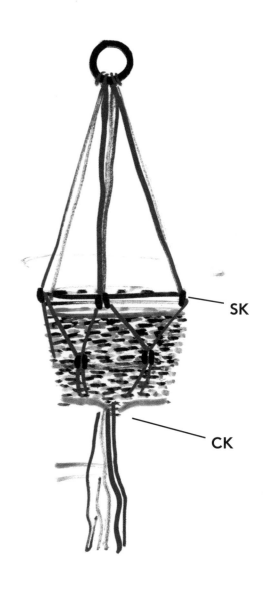

Bike basket

I love cycling in the city and wanted to add a bit of a fun to my bike with this basket. The autumnal green and orange colours are inspired by my favourite season for riding my bike.

Materials:
Pre-drilled oval basket base with 42 holes*
4 pieces of 2.65mm (⁷⁄₆₄ inch) centre cane
   (see the chart on page 75 regarding cane
   sizes), each piece needs to be at least
   1m (39 inches)
Bucket of lukewarm water, plus a towel
30m (33 yards) of orange twine
100m (110 yards) of green jute twine
Measuring tape
Masking tape
Large-eyed needle
Pegs or small clips
Leather straps with buckles

* If you can't find a basket base, create your own with an oval piece of plywood 30cm (12 inches) long x 20cm (8 inches) wide, and drill 42 holes evenly spaced around the edge.

The basket

1. Soak 2 x 1-m (39-inch) lengths of cane in a bucket of lukewarm water for 5 minutes so it's flexible (see page 91).

2. Working from the back of the basket base, thread the first piece of cane up from the base and then back down, skipping one hole and creating a loop 20cm (8 inches) high.

3. Bring the cane back up through the base, again skipping one hole and repeat the process until you have created looped stakes around the entire base – you should have 10 loops in total and 20 stakes.

4. Finishing by threading what you have left of the cane through the undersides of the stakes.

5. Cut 2 x 1-m (39-inch) lengths of orange twine – these will act as the 2 weavers.

6. Join in the first weaver by tying a double knot to one of the cane stakes, then feed it down through the hole to its right and back up through the next hole.

Tip: Wrap a short piece of masking tape around the end of your twine (like a shoelace) to make it easier to thread through the holes.

7. Join in the second weaver by tying a double knot to the stake immediately to the right of the first weaver. Take the second weaver immediately behind the stake to its right and feed it down through the hole immediately after and back up through the next hole. Then work anti-clockwise by going in front of the stake immediately to your left, behind the next one. The second weaver is now back next to the first weaver.

8. Take the first weaver in front of the next stake and behind it, then repeat with the second weaver (see step 2, page 126).

9. Take the first weaver in front of the next stake and feed it down through the hole right next to it and feed it back up through the next hole to the right.

10. Repeat every time you reach an empty hole until none are left on your base.

11. You have now secured your twine to the base and can weave rows of pairing in orange as normal (see step 2, page 126).

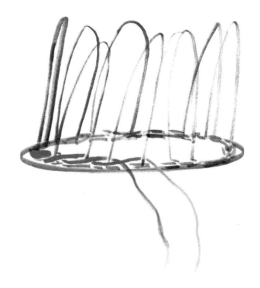

To make vertical stripes instead of horizontal ones, simply work with 2 weavers of different colours!

12. If you need to join in new twine, simply tie a new length to the end of your weaver, using a double knot and with the knot on the inside of the basket.

13. When your orange weaving is about 5cm (2 inches) high, change colour (see step 6, page 128). Join 2 x 2-m (2¼-yard) lengths of green twine to your 2 orange weavers and continue pairing until you have a few centimetres (inches) left on your stakes. You might want use pegs or small clips to hold your stakes in the right position.

The rim

14. To create the rim of your basket, thread the remaining pieces of cane through your stakes, going in and out of each. Make sure you soak your cane first so it is pliable (see page 91). These pieces of cane act as a border and will help to prevent your rows of pairing unravelling.

16. When your first weaver reaches the second weaver at the end of row 3, unthread it from the needle. Join your 2 weavers together on the inside of the basket with a double knot. Trim off any ends.

17. Finish by threading the leather straps between your top row of pairing and the rim (you might have to re-adjust them to suit to the handlebars of your bike).

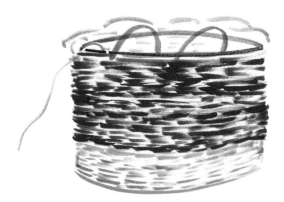

15. Thread the remaining twine of your first weaver into the needle and start wrapping it around the stakes and the rim. Continue working around the basket. You will need to complete at least 3 rows of wrapping to ensure the rim is secured.

Suppliers

This is a list of suppliers I've been relying on for the projects in this book. All items are available online but if you do have the opportunity to buy them in person, please do so to familiarize yourself with the textures and double-check that materials are of good quality.

Grasses
Your local garden centre, or:

British Wild Flower Plants
wildflowers.co.uk

Jacksons Nurseries
jacksonsnurseries.co.uk

Gardening Express
gardeningexpress.co.uk

Plastic strings
Search for 'scoubidou' or plastic lacing string on amazon.co.uk or amazon.com

Cane and cane tools
Fred Aldous
fredaldous.co.uk

Somerset Willow Growers
willowgrowers.co.uk

Cotton rope
MacCulloch & Wallis
macculloch-wallis.co.uk

Ray-Stitch
raystitch.co.uk

Joann
joann.com

Rolls of jute twine and sisal
Nutscene
nutscene.com

Kent & Stowe
kentandstowe.com

Fabric dyes
Rit
ritdye.com

Lampholder with switched cable and fitted plug
amazon.co.uk or amazon.com

Leather or jeans needles and extra-strength thread
Your local haberdashery shop

Basket base with pre-drilled holes
Fred Aldous
fredaldous.co.uk

Bike straps
Etsy
etsy.com

Bobbin Bikes
bobbinbikes.com

Additional tools
Your local craft shop

Index

Bibliography

Meilach, Dona Z, *A Modern Approach to Basketry With Fibers and Grasses* (Crown Publishers, 1974)
Rosengarten, Dale, *Grass Roots: African Origins of an American Art* (Museum for African Art, 2008)
Wright, Dorothy, *The Complete Book of Basketry* (David and Charles, 1992)

Acknowledgements

As I sit down to write this note, I'm so grateful to have so many wonderful people in my life who have been part of this journey with me.

I'd like to start by thanking my family who have supported me every step of the way – sorry I've been MIA for the past year while 'I was writing a book'. I love you all and I can't wait for you to see this beauty.

Troels – my partner in crime, my 'assistant', this book is as much yours as it is mine. Thank you for holding my hand every day and making me believe I could do it during moments of doubt. I'm so grateful to have you in my life.

To my dear friend Victoria, who's been with me on this crazy journey from my book proposal to the finished item you're holding today. You've been amazing throughout this whole process and I'm so thankful for our friendship. I can't wait to see what the future brings to you.

To my friends, my girls, my best friends – I'm back! Thank you all for being so understanding, kind and supportive.

I could not have asked for a better team to work on this book and would like to thank the dreamy duo of Harriet and Gemma for their guidance, patience and support, the rest of the team at Quadrille/Hardie Grant for their work on this book, and everybody else involved in this project.

Penny – it has been a long dream of mine to work with you and I'm so happy and in awe of the beautiful work you've created. So effortless, so cool! Thank you.

Sidy – thank you for travelling miles and miles away from Dakar to beautifully capture the girls – your photos are now travelling the world. You're so talented and generous. *Merci mon ami.*

To all the loyal customers of La Basketry who are supporting a small business – every order and every word of encouragement means the world. Here's to more happy dances!

Last but not least, there would be no book without the artisans I'm humbled to work with – thank you for teaching me, inspiring me, thank you for trusting Mamy and me. I'm proud to continue to shine light on the beautiful work you're doing.